GREAT MINDS THINK DIFFERENTLY

Quotes and Affirmations to Celebrate the Power of Neurodiversity

summersdale

GREAT MINDS THINK DIFFERENTLY

Compiled by Amanda Marples

An Hachette UK Company
www.hachette.co.uk

Summersdale Publishers
Part of Octopus Publishing Group Limited
Carmelite House
50 Victoria Embankment
LONDON
EC4Y 0DZ
UK

www.summersdale.com

This FSC® label means that materials and other controlled sources used for the product have been responsibly sourced

FSC www.fsc.org MIX Paper | Supporting responsible forestry FSC® C016973

The authorized representative in the EEA is Hachette Ireland, 8 Castlecourt Centre, Dublin 15, D15 XTP3, Ireland (email: info@hbgi.ie)

Printed and bound in China

ISBN: 978-1-83799-478-6
eISBN: 978-1-83799-544-8

TO..................................

FROM..............................

INTRODUCTION

A brain that is not wired in the "regular" way comes with extraordinary gifts of creativity, innovation and passion. Congratulations if you own a brain like this! But you may also find the neurotypical world lonely and difficult at times. This uplifting collection of affirmations and quotes from those who embrace different ways of thinking and being in the world – some neurodivergent and some not – will help you recognize your own unique brilliance and unleash the power of your mind. Here you will be reminded that different does not mean less. It's time to celebrate the incredible diversity of the human mind!

I AM PROUD OF MY DIFFERENCES

Neurodiversity may be every bit as crucial for the human race as biodiversity is for life in general. Who can say what form of wiring will be best at any given moment?

HARVEY BLUME

BEING DIFFERENT
MEANS BEING UNIQUE
AND THAT'S WHAT MAKES
THE WORLD AN EXCITING
PLACE TO BE IN.

A. J. ODUDU

By looking at autistic women I admired I began to realize that an autistic brain could provide an escape route from the traditional paths laid out for women.

FERN BRADY

MY THINKING STYLE IS UNIQUE AND BEAUTIFUL

Autism is as much a part
of humanity as is the
capacity to dream.

KATHLEEN SEIDEL

"NORMAL" IS A DRYER SETTING.

ELIZABETH MOON

INCLUSION MATTERS

I am wired a completely different way and I'm only just understanding it. Where I used to think "what's wrong with me?" now I know it's everything that's right with me.

MELANIE SYKES

SUCCESS IS TO BE
MEASURED NOT SO MUCH
BY THE POSITION THAT
ONE HAS REACHED IN LIFE
AS BY THE OBSTACLES
WHICH HE HAS OVERCOME.

BOOKER T. WASHINGTON

A diagnosis is not a prediction. It doesn't tell you what's possible... It just opens up tricks and tools to thrive.

JOLENE STOCKMAN

I CAN ASK FOR MY NEEDS TO BE MET

I will not be erased. I am proud, I am loud, I am powerful beyond belief.

BEX TAYLOR-KLAUS

NORMAL IS OVERRATED.

LISA ARO

I DO NOT
HAVE TO MAKE
MYSELF FIT IN

If it weren't for Asperger's and obsessions there would be no Theory of Relativity, no *Magic Flute*, no Microsoft... and no *Ghost Busters*.

RUDY SIMONE

ADHD ISN'T A BAD THING, AND YOU SHOULDN'T FEEL DIFFERENT FROM THOSE WITHOUT ADHD. REMEMBER THAT YOU ARE NOT ALONE.

ADAM LEVINE

If it weren't for my struggle with dyslexia, I doubt I'd ever have become a writer or known how to teach others to write.

PHILIP SCHULTZ

THE

WORLD NEEDS

THINKERS WHO

DIVERGE FROM

THE NORM

It was such a turning point to find that I had a talent and I had something to contribute, somewhere.

GWEN STEFANI

WE NEED DIVERSITY OF THOUGHT IN THE WORLD TO FACE THE NEW CHALLENGES.

TIM BERNERS-LEE

I CAN MAKE MY ENVIRONMENT WORK FOR ME

It is time for parents to teach young people early on that in diversity there is beauty and there is strength.

MAYA ANGELOU

RELISH EVERYTHING THAT'S INSIDE OF YOU, THE IMPERFECTIONS, THE DARKNESS, THE RICHNESS AND LIGHT AND EVERYTHING.

ANTHONY HOPKINS

We are acceptable humans as is, not once we stop having ADHD. You do not need to be fixed because you are not a broken version of normal.

JESSICA McCABE

MY CHALLENGES
DO NOT DEFINE ME

You need to give what's best in you a chance to grow with the right gardener, one who sees that you're a special plant, not a weed.

EDWARD HALLOWELL

OUR ABILITY
TO REACH UNITY IN
DIVERSITY WILL BE THE
BEAUTY AND THE TEST
OF OUR CIVILIZATION.

MAHATMA GANDHI

ASKING FOR
HELP IS NOT
A WEAKNESS

Tell the world you are a one-of-a-kind creation who came here to experience wonder and spread joy. Expect to be accommodated.

VICTORIA MORAN

SOMETIMES,
THE MOST BRILLIANT
AND INTELLIGENT
MINDS DO NOT SHINE
IN STANDARDIZED
TESTS BECAUSE THEY
DO NOT HAVE
STANDARDIZED MINDS.

DIANE RAVITCH

Creativity is the key for any child with dyslexia – or for anyone, for that matter. Then you can think outside of the box.

ORLANDO BLOOM

I AM GOOD
ENOUGH JUST
AS I AM

Creativity has helped me transform myself from a Tourette's "sufferer" into a Tourette's superhero.

JESS THOM

THE HUMAN BRAIN IS AS DIVERSE AS THE HUMAN FINGERPRINT.

VICTORIA McGOVERN

BEING ALONE IS TOTALLY ACCEPTABLE IF THAT IS WHAT I NEED

Refusing to perform neurotypicality is a revolutionary act of disability justice. It's also a radical act of self-love.

DEVON PRICE

DYSLEXIA, THOUGH, MADE ME REALIZE THAT PEOPLE WHO SAY "BUT YOU CAN'T DO THAT" AREN'T ACTUALLY VERY IMPORTANT. I DON'T TAKE "NO" TOO SERIOUSLY.

RICHARD ROGERS

The only thing breaking me was pretending to be like everyone else.

KATHERINE MAY

I TRUST MY
INNER VOICE

To measure the success of our societies, we should examine how well those with different abilities, including persons with autism, are integrated as full and valued members.

BAN KI-MOON

AS ARE MOST KIDS WHO HAVE ADHD, MINE WERE BRILLIANT, TALENTED AND CHARMING.

DIANE BAUMER

EVERYTHING I
NEED IS ALREADY
WITHIN ME

Diversity:
the art of thinking
independently
together.

MALCOLM S. FORBES

ASPERGER'S DOESN'T DEFINE ME. IT'S A CONDITION THAT I HAVE TO LIVE WITH AND WORK THROUGH.

SUSAN BOYLE

A breakdown led to me getting diagnosed and it was the best possible thing for me – it has allowed me to understand my strengths and weaknesses.

JORDAN CATCHPOLE

I FORM CONNECTIONS WITH OTHERS IN MY OWN WAY

You're only given a
little spark of madness.
You mustn't lose it.

ROBIN WILLIAMS

WITHOUT DEVIATION FROM THE NORM, PROGRESS IS NOT POSSIBLE.

FRANK ZAPPA

WE ALL
DESERVE TO
BE HEARD

You have something unique that no one else has – your life experience. That's the power of you.

MEL ROBBINS

THE MOST INTERESTING PEOPLE YOU'LL FIND ARE ONES THAT DON'T FIT INTO YOUR AVERAGE CARDBOARD BOX. THEY'LL MAKE WHAT THEY NEED, THEY'LL MAKE THEIR OWN BOXES.

TEMPLE GRANDIN

I would never wish
to be any other way
than my awesome
self. I love being me,
regardless of the early
challenges I had faced.

SCOTT SONNON

NEURODIVERGENCE IS ONLY ONE PART OF ME

You don't need the
world to understand you.
It's fine. Some people will
never really understand things
they haven't experienced.

MATT HAIG

I SEE PEOPLE WITH ASPERGER'S SYNDROME AS A BRIGHT THREAD IN THE RICH TAPESTRY OF LIFE.

TONY ATTWOOD

I CAN TAKE UP SPACE IN THE WORLD

I'm on the autism spectrum. I don't usually follow social coding and so therefore I go my own way.

GRETA THUNBERG

THE ADHD SIDE OF ME DOES LEAD TO CERTAIN DISORGANIZATION AND CHAOS IN MY LIFE, AND I HAVE MANY FLAWS AND THINGS I'M BAD AT, BUT I'M QUITE GOOD AT GETTING BACK UP AGAIN.

RICHARD BACON

Identifying as neurodivergent isn't just another label; it's also an identity, it's a reclamation, it's a song.

SONNY JANE WISE

MY LIFE STRATEGIES ARE STRONG AND EFFECTIVE

I AM WORTHY OF COMPASSION

What I would tell a kid with ADHD and dyslexia or someone who struggles with anything in life is this: "When you put your mind to it, you can do anything."

MICHELLE CARTER

DEFICITS AND DISABILITIES ONLY EXIST IN RELATION TO AN ENVIRONMENT WHERE SOME OTHER WAY OF FUNCTIONING HAS BEEN CHOSEN AS THE YARDSTICK.

CLARA TÖRNVALL

Diversity drives innovation – when we limit who can contribute, we in turn limit what problems we can solve.

TELLE WHITNEY

MY MIND TAKES ME TO INCREDIBLE PLACES

Dyslexic kids are creative,
"outside-the-box" thinkers.
They have to be, because they
don't see or solve problems
the same way other kids do.

RICK RIORDAN

NEURODIVERSITY IS THE FUTURE OF INNOVATION AND PROGRESS.

STEVE SILBERMAN

I'M HAPPY TO
BE EXACTLY
WHO I AM

For me, in my life,
dyslexia has been a
little bit of a blessing.
It helped me find my
strength and directed
me towards what I
really wanted to do.

DARCEY BUSSELL

IT DOES NOT MATTER
WHAT 66 PER CENT
OF PEOPLE DO IN ANY
PARTICULAR SITUATION.
ALL THAT MATTERS IS
WHAT YOU DO.

JOHN ELDER ROBISON

Neurodiversity is the art of celebrating the unique wiring of every brain.

CORINA LYNN BECKER

MY BOUNDARIES MATTER

I have Tourette's and Asperger's, but Tourette's and Asperger's don't have me.

JAMES DURBIN

AUTISM ISN'T AN ILLNESS. IT'S A DIFFERENT WAY OF BEING HUMAN.

BARRY M. PRIZANT

I LOVE MY UNIQUE BRAIN

I think being different, going against the grain of society is the greatest thing in the world.

ELIJAH WOOD

I WAS BUILT THIS WAY FOR A REASON, SO I'M GOING TO USE IT.

SIMONE BILES

My definition of cool is finding your own definition of cool and not necessarily taking your lead from what other people tell you.

WENTWORTH MILLER

I RESPECT MY
NEED FOR REST

The only disability is
when people cannot see
human potential.

DEBRA RUH

NEURODIVERSITY IS NOT ABOUT BEING "NORMAL". IT'S ABOUT BEING YOUR AUTHENTIC SELF.

DAVID FINCH

DIFFERENCE DOES NOT MEAN DEFICIT

I don't want other people to decide who I am. I want to decide that for myself.

EMMA WATSON

I'M NOT A TYPICAL AUTISTIC PERSON, BECAUSE THERE IS NO TYPICAL AUTISTIC PERSON.

CHRIS PACKHAM

Neurodiversity is not just a matter of social justice, it is a matter of Human rights.

JUDY SINGER

I AM COMPETENT AND CAPABLE

We do not need
to cure neurodiversity.
We need to embrace it.

JONATHAN MOONEY

NEURODIVERSITY MAY BE THE BIRTHPLACE OF SOME OF HUMANITY'S GREATEST MINDS.

HARVEY BLUME

MY MENTAL
HEALTH IS
A PRIORITY

My thoughts are disordered, not especially logical, and not at all linear, but that's OK – they take me to more interesting places.

FLORENCE WELCH

WE EXIST, FULL STOP,
NO QUALIFIERS NEEDED.

EMILY PAIGE BALLOU

The privilege of a
lifetime is being
who you are.

JOSEPH CAMPBELL

I AM PROUD OF
WHO I AM

Surround yourself with only people who are going to lift you higher.

OPRAH WINFREY

I AM NATURALLY SOLITARY, AND I'M COMFORTABLE WITH THAT.

ANNE HEGERTY

SENSITIVITY IS A VALUABLE ASSET

I take on too much and end up spinning plates, but it's entertaining, and it helps you make quick connections if you're a comedian, if you have a brain that can dance around too much.

RORY BREMNER

BEING DIFFERENT GIVES THE WORLD COLOUR.

NELSAN ELLIS

Normal is not something to aspire to, it's something to get away from.

JODIE FOSTER

I CAN TRUST
MY INTUITION

Being different and
thinking differently make
a person unforgettable.

SUZY KASSEM

AUTISM IS NOT A TRAGEDY. IGNORANCE IS THE REAL TRAGEDY.

TEMPLE GRANDIN

I DESERVE UNDERSTANDING

What makes a child gifted and talented may not always be good grades in school, but a different way of looking at the world and learning.

CHUCK GRASSLEY

WE SHOULD CELEBRATE NEURODIVERSITY – THE WORLD WOULD BE POORER AND LIFE DULLER IF WE WERE ALL THE SAME.

NEIL MILLIKEN

Here's to the crazy ones. The misfits. The rebels. The troublemakers. The round pegs in the square holes. The ones who see things differently.

STEVE JOBS

WE ALL MATTER

We as a society need the millions of neurodiverse children in the world today, with their powerful gifts, talents, and abilities, to flourish. Because they are the future.

DEBORAH REBER

DIVERSITY IS CRITICAL TO INNOVATION.

JULIE SWEET

MY

DIFFERENCES

DO NOT HOLD

ME BACK

Autism doesn't have to define a person. Artists with autism are like anyone else: they define themselves through hard work and individuality.

ADRIENNE BAILON

BEING A POET,
THE ADVANTAGES OF
DYSLEXIA ARE MANY,
AFFORDING ME SENSITIVITY
TO THE MUSICAL NUANCES OF
LANGUAGE AND THE ABILITY
TO JUGGLE COMPLICATED
IDEAS AND NARRATIVES
SIMULTANEOUSLY.

PHILIP SCHULTZ

THINKING DIFFERENTLY HAS GIVEN ME THE TOOLS TO FACE CHAOS AND FAILURE.

KAIYA STONE

I DO NOT NEED TO JUSTIFY MY NEEDS

We are different because our brain is wired differently. This causes us to perceive the world in different ways and have different values and priorities. Not better or worse – different.

ALLAN PEASE

YOU DON'T HAVE TRUE FREEDOM UNTIL YOU ALLOW A DIVERSITY OF OPINION AND A DIVERSITY OF VOICES.

DON LEMON

I CREATE ROUTINES THAT WORK FOR ME

To change the world, you must be different than the world. To lead, you must go first. You must divert from the common path, you must navigate unmapped terrain.

BRIANNA WIEST

I LIKE THAT I HAVE TEN THINGS ON THE GO, ALL AT ONCE. I LIKE THAT I'M ALWAYS PLANNING FOR THE NEXT THING. I LIKE THAT I BRING A HIGH ENERGY TO MY LIFE, THAT I SEE IT AS A CHALLENGE.

EMILIE PINE

It took 24 years for me to harness my autistic traits into something useful, and I have grown to regard them as a kind of superpower.

JACK MONROE

ALL

PERSPECTIVES

ARE VALID

You see, we're not hyperactive,
just otherworldly energetic.
We're not distractible,
just incessantly curious.

TRACY OTSUKA

FAULT! ASPERGER'S ISN'T A FAULT. IT'S A VARIANT. IT'S POTENTIALLY A MAJOR ADVANTAGE.

GRAEME SIMSION

I AM ALLOWED
TO TAKE BREAKS

We refuse to conform.
We refuse to comply.
We are beautiful and
unique. We are never
going to go away,
and we are going to
change the world.

BEVERLY L. ANDERSON

IF A PERSON'S BEHAVIOUR DOESN'T MAKE SENSE TO YOU, IT IS BECAUSE YOU ARE MISSING A PART OF THEIR CONTEXT. IT'S THAT SIMPLE.

DEVON PRICE

There are enough people in the world who are going to write you off. You don't need to do that to yourself.

SUSAN BOYLE

I KNOW
MY WORTH

We should indeed keep calm in the face of difference, and live our lives in a state of inclusion and wonder at the diversity of humanity.

GEORGE TAKEI

WHEN YOU DANCE TO YOUR OWN RHYTHM, LIFE TAPS ITS TOES TO YOUR BEAT.

TERRI GUILLEMETS

I AM AT PEACE WITH MYSELF

People with ADHD often have a special feel for life, a way of seeing right into the heart of matters.

EDWARD HALLOWELL

SOME OF THE SMARTEST PEOPLE IN THE WORLD, MAJOR OWNERS OF COMPANIES, ARE DYSLEXIC. WE JUST SEE THINGS DIFFERENTLY, SO THAT'S AN ADVANTAGE.

CHARLOTTE McKINNEY

It's important to
me that people can
associate being different
with being beautiful.

ANDREJ PEJIC

I ACCEPT ALL
MY EMOTIONAL
REACTIONS

Out in the real world, my dyslexia became my massive advantage: it helped me to think creatively and laterally, and see solutions where others saw problems.

RICHARD BRANSON

I THOUGHT NOT FITTING IN WAS SOMETHING I HAD TO FIX. NOW I SEE IT AS MY SUPERPOWER.

MAXIME LAGACÉ

THERE ARE MANY WAYS TO EXPRESS FEELINGS

Being different is awesome! All of those who are different are more interesting than those who are clamouring for acceptance because they follow the path.

TONY HAWK

UNITY, NOT UNIFORMITY,
MUST BE OUR AIM.
WE ATTAIN UNITY ONLY
THROUGH VARIETY.
DIFFERENCES MUST
BE INTEGRATED,
NOT ANNIHILATED,
NOT ABSORBED.

MARY PARKER FOLLETT

Nobody is superior,
nobody is inferior, but
nobody is equal either.
People are simply
unique, incomparable.
You are you, I am I.

OSHO

CONFORMITY IS LIMITING

I'm very proud of my dyslexia.
I wouldn't have it any other way.
It sits absolutely with what I do,
how I think, and who I am.

JAMES WILLIAM MIDDLETON

IF YOU ARE ALWAYS TRYING TO BE NORMAL, YOU WILL NEVER KNOW HOW AMAZING YOU CAN BE.

MAYA ANGELOU

THERE IS STRENGTH
IN BEING UNIQUE

To be yourself
in a world that is
constantly trying to
make you something
else is the greatest
accomplishment.

RALPH WALDO EMERSON

HAVING ADHD, AND TAKING MEDICINE FOR IT IS NOTHING TO BE ASHAMED OF, NOTHING THAT I'M AFRAID TO LET PEOPLE KNOW.

SIMONE BILES

Our brains are
sending sparks in
different directions and
sometimes they end
up in the wrong place,
but sometimes they end
up in incredible places.

CHARLOTTE AMELIA POE

GREAT
MINDS THINK
DIFFERENTLY

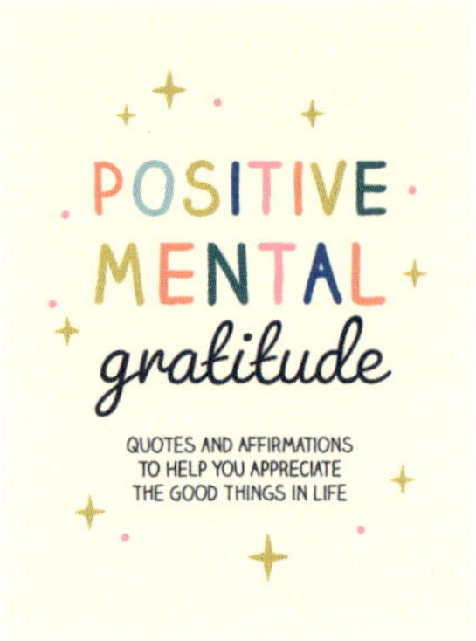

Positive Mental Gratitude

Quotes and Affirmations to Help You Appreciate the Good Things in Life

Hardback | 978-1-80007-836-9

This gentle book – spilling over with beautiful quotes and statements on the practice of gratitude – will empower you to celebrate the present, even in times of challenge and change

Gratitude is a gift that never stops giving. Helping you to see wonderful moments in the everyday, strengthen your relationships and improve your health, practising gratitude can boost your spirits and drive positive change.

You Are So Awesome

Uplifting Quotes and Affirmations to
Celebrate How Amazing You Are

Hardback | 978-1-83799-353-6

Be proud of who you are with the help of these inspirational quotes and empowering affirmations

If you're feeling down or need some encouragement, this pocket-sized book of positive quotes and powerful affirmations will help show you how great you are. These inspiring words are here to remind you that there is no one quite like you, and your uniqueness is what makes you amazing.

Have you enjoyed this book?
If so, find us on Facebook
at **Summersdale Publishers**,
on Twitter/X at **@Summersdale**
and on Instagram and TikTok at
@summersdalebooks and get in
touch. We'd love to hear from you!

www.summersdale.com

Image credits
pp.8, 15, 22, 29, 36, 43, 50, 57, 64, 71, 78, 85, 92, 99, 106, 113, 120, 127, 134, 141, 148, 155 – lines © avian/Shutterstock.com